Global Issues

Natural Resources

Cheryl Jakab

Smart Apple Media

Smart Apple Media
2140 Howard Drive West
North Mankato, Minnesota 56003

First published in 2007 by
MACMILLAN EDUCATION AUSTRALIA PTY LTD
627 Chapel Street, South Yarra, Australia 3141

Visit our Web site at www.macmillan.com.au or go directly to www.macmillanlibrary.com.au

Associated companies and representatives throughout the world.

Copyright © Cheryl Jakab 2007

Library of Congress Cataloging-in-Publication Data

Jakab, Cheryl.
    Natural resources / by Cheryl Jakab.
    p. cm. — (Global issues)
    Includes index.
    ISBN 978-1-59920-125-2
    1. Conservation of natural resources—Juvenile literature. I. Title.

    S940.J35 2007
    333.7—dc22

                                                    2007004561

Edited by Anna Fern
Text and cover design by Cristina Neri, Canary Graphic Design
Page layout by Domenic Lauricella and Cristina Neri
Photo research by Legend Images
Illustrations by Andrew Louey; maps courtesy of Geo Atlas

Printed in U.S.

Acknowledgements
The author and the publisher are grateful to the following for permission to reproduce copyright material:

Front cover inset photograph: Truck and loader at mining face for bauxite, Weipa, Queensland, Australia, © Photolibrary. Earth photograph courtesy of Photodisc.

Background photograph of Earth and magnifying glass image both courtesy of Photodisc.

Alcan Gove, p. 14; BigStockPhoto, pp. 7 (bottom), 8, 12, 23; Corbis/Australian Picture Library/Viviane Moos, pp. 7 (right), 17; © Bedo/Dreamstime.com, p. 19; © Karimala/Dreamstime.com, p. 20; © Kwerry/Dreamstime. com, p. 16; © Photoneer/Dreamstime.com, pp. 6 (top), 24; © Pryzmat /Dreamstime.com, p. 26 ; Andrew De La Rue/Fairfaxphotos, p. 15; © Klementiev/Fotolia, p. 9; © Anita Patterson Peppers/Fotolia, p. 22; © Francisco Putini/ Fotolia, p. 18; Louisa Gouliamaki/AFP/Getty Images, p. 25; National Geographic/Getty Images, pp. 6 (bottom), 13; Monash Asia Institute, photo by Lea Jellinek, p. 27; NOAA, pp. 6 (left), 21; Photolibrary, pp. 5, 29; © emin kuliyev/ Shutterstock, p. 11.

While every care has been taken to trace and acknowledge copyright, the publisher tenders their apologies for any accidental infringement where copyright has proved untraceable. Where the attempt has been unsuccessful, the publisher welcomes information that would redress the situation.

Please note
At the time of printing, the Internet addresses appearing in this book were correct. Owing to the dynamic nature of the Internet, however, we cannot guarantee that all these addresses will remain correct.

Contents

Glossary words
When a word is printed in **bold**, you can look up its meaning in the glossary on page 31.

Facing global issues

Hi there! This is Earth speaking. Will you take a moment to listen to me? I have some very important things to discuss.

We must face up to some urgent environmental problems! All living things depend on my environment, but the way you humans are living at the moment, I will not be able to keep looking after you.

The issues I am worried about are:
- the huge number of people on Earth
- the supply of clean air and water
- wasting resources
- energy supplies for the future
- protecting all living things
- **global warming** and **climate change**

My global challenge to you is to find a **sustainable** way of living. Read on to find out what people around the world are doing to try to help.

Fast fact

In 2005, the United Nations Environment Program Report, written by experts from 95 countries, concluded that 60 percent of Earth's resources are being **degraded** or used unsustainably.

What's the issue?
Managing natural resources

Natural resources are the materials people take from Earth to make products. The supply of natural resources must be managed so it does not run out.

Manufactured products

Natural resources are needed to manufacture all the products people use every day, such as glass, plastic, metals, paper, and lumber. Manufactured items, including computers, cars, shoes, and carpets, and all the containers and packaging they come in, are made from natural resources.

Resources and the environment

Natural resources are valuable. Their use can help make life easier and more comfortable. It is important to realize that:

- the supply of natural resources is limited and can run out
- many resources are rare or hard to get
- it takes money and energy to supply resources
- taking and using resources damages the environment

Fast fact
A 50-ton pile of ore is needed to produce just four ounces (113 g) of pure platinum.

There is a limit to the natural resources that Earth can supply.

Natural resources issues

The most urgent issues with natural resources around the globe include:
- high rates of **consumption** (see issue 1)
- damage from mining (see issue 2)
- lumber harvesting decreasing forest cover (see issue 3)
- loss of soil fertility and **erosion** (see issue 4)
- throwing away resources as garbage (see issue 5)

Arctic Circle

NORTH

AMERICA
United States

NORTH

ATLANT

OCEAN

SOUTH

AMERICA

A T

O

ISSUE 4

United States
Soil erosion and decrease in soil fertility. See pages 20–23.

ISSUE 2

South Africa
Damage to the environment from mining. See pages 12–15.

around the globe

ISSUE 5

Greece
Natural resources going to waste. See pages 24–27.

ISSUE 3

Indonesia
Unsustainable logging of forests. See pages 16–19.

EUROPE

Greece

ASIA

AFRICA

Arctic Circle

Indonesia

Equator

AUSTRALIA

Tropic of Capricorn

South Africa

UTH

NTIC

EAN

ANTARCTICA

ISSUE 1

Australia
A high-consumption society. See pages 8–11.

Overconsumption of natural resources

Today, consumption of natural resources in many countries is racing out of control. Many high-consuming societies ignore the long-term effects of overconsumption.

Consumers consuming

Consumers are the people who buy and consume goods. Consumers purchase many items that make their lives better, easier, and more comfortable. As standards of living increase, consumption per person also increases, houses get larger, and purchasing of luxury items increases. Supplying these goods uses up enormous amounts of natural resources each year.

Manufacturing and the environment

Each stage of production of every item causes some environmental damage. Damage occurs in mining or growing resources, in manufacture, transportation, and disposal after use. Many industrial processes add to environmental degradation by land clearing, soil erosion, or pollution with toxic wastes.

Fast fact

People in industrial "consumer societies" account for about 20 percent of world population, yet use most of the world's supplies, including:
- aluminum (86 percent)
- paper (81 percent)
- iron and steel (80 percent)
- lumber (76 percent)

Levels of consumption in developed countries are racing out of control.

Plastic shopping bags and packaging create huge litter problems.

CASE STUDY
Australians and plastic shopping bags

Australian consumption of natural resources per person is 20 to 24 times that of people living in the poorest countries. The disposable plastic shopping bag has become a symbol of Australia's high consumption of manufactured goods and also creates huge garbage problems.

Billions of bags

In 2004, Australians used one disposable plastic shopping bag for every person in the country for every day of the year! Most of the 5.6 billion bags used each year are high-density polyethylene (HDPE) bags, the type used in supermarkets. This figure does not even take into account other plastic bags, such as those used for fruits and vegetables. Most plastics, including plastic bags, are made from oil. These plastics use up resources and create a huge garbage problem.

Alternatives are available

Many alternatives to the plastic shopping bag are available, such as reusable cloth bags. With a little planning, people can easily take their own bags with them when they go shopping.

Toward a sustainable future: Reducing consumption

Reducing levels of consumption is one way to help conserve natural resources. Individuals, manufacturers, and organizations are all working on ways to reduce consumption.

The ecological footprint

In the 1990s, Canadian Bill Rees developed the idea of the ecological footprint to show how many resources people used. The ecological footprint is a calculation of how much land is needed to produce all the resources and energy people use. It is a way individuals, businesses, and society can compare resource use, and think about ways consumption can be reduced.

Changing manufacturing

Devising better ways to manufacture can help reduce environmental impacts. Environmentally friendly manufacturing, or "eco-design," aims to:

- reduce the amount of material and energy used in the product
- reduce toxic materials produced and released in production
- increase **recycling** and reuse of products
- extend the life of products

Eco-design reviews each step of the product "life cycle."

Could we use recycled materials instead?

Getting **raw materials** and transporting them

How much pollution is produced?

Processing

Can we use less packaging?

Distribution and sales

Will this product last a long time?

Consumer use

Can the packaging be recycled?

Disposal

Billboards and other advertising encourage consumption of resources.

CASE STUDY
Advertising and consumption

Advertising is used throughout the world to promote the sale of products and services. Huge signs in lights, billboards, television, magazines, and newspapers bombard people with advertising every day. Today, advertising is very cleverly designed and targeted to maximize its effectiveness.

Understanding effects of advertising on purchasing can help reduce consumption. Advertising can be useful in telling people about products, but it also encourages, tempts and convinces people to buy more and more. Individuals need to think "Do I really need it?" before they buy.

Fast fact
Some studies suggest resource use in high consuming societies needs to be reduced by as much as 90 percent in the next 20 years to be sustainable.

Advertising works

Advertising can make people more likely to buy a product. People today need to be more aware of the role of advertising and the messages it uses to sell items. This can help develop "sales resistance" which can reduce overconsumption of resources.

Consumer organizations can help people make informed choices. Campaigns such as "International Buy Nothing Day" encourage people to resist advertising and be more conscious of their consumption.

Mining natural resources

Mining is the process of taking natural resources from the ground. Mining can be carried out on Earth's surface and underground. It is not possible to mine without damaging the environment in some way.

What is mined?

Mined materials include all the metals we use every day. **Fossil fuels** such as coal and oil, minerals such as quartz, and building materials including sand, gravel, clays, and limestone are all mined. These resources are **nonrenewable**.

Metals from mining	
precious metals	gold, silver, platinum
steel industry metals	iron, nickel
base metals	copper, lead, tin, zinc
light metals	magnesium, aluminum
radioactive metals	uranium
specialty metals	lithium, arsenic

Damage from mining

Mining is considered to be one of the biggest causes of environmental damage worldwide. Today damage caused by mining includes:

- huge amounts of soil and rock moved each year, increasing erosion
- release of toxic materials
- production of huge piles of "tailings," or wastes, which remain unsuitable as habitat for hundreds of years
- use of huge amounts of energy

About 60 percent of mining is done in open-cut mines, such as this one in Quebec, Canada.

These huge waste heaps in Johannesburg, South Africa are a reminder of damage caused by gold mining in the past.

CASE STUDY
Mining in South Africa

South Africa is very rich in mineral resources, which provide two-thirds of the country's exports. Gold, diamonds, and coal are the most important. Other products of South Africa's mines include platinum, iron ore, chromium, limestone, asbestos, uranium, copper, lead, silver, and zinc.

Most of the mining in South Africa has had huge environmental impacts. Disturbance of the surface of the ground and pollution associated with mining are among the most serious environmental threats in South Africa.

Open-pit mining

Most mining in South Africa is by open pit. The diamond mines of South Africa are examples of terraced pits, which go deeper and deeper into the earth. Open-pit mines get larger in area as they go down. Permanently scarred areas and heaps of waste from mines in South Africa are evidence of the damage caused by mining.

Fast fact
As well as damaging the environment, mining in South Africa in the past developed with little care for worker safety or sharing of the profits with the workers.

13

Toward a sustainable future: Sustainable mining

Mined resources will continue to be needed in the future. Care needs to be taken in every step of mining natural resources. Environmental awareness is necessary to develop a more sustainable mining industry.

Regulation of mining

Regulations controlling mining operations can reduce the environmental impacts of mining. Modern mining designed by qualified engineers that considers the environment has much less impact.

Before mining, companies in some countries are required to carry out "environmental impact studies." These show how the company plans to carry out the mining while protecting the land. Restoring the site after mining, by replacing rock, soil, and vegetation, is part of the process. This may make mining more difficult or costly, but is designed to be less damaging and safer.

Fast fact

Mined resources, such as aluminum and other metals, can be reused and recycled to help conserve supplies.

Traditional owners and mining

When areas rich in resources are mined, the rights of traditional owners of the land need to be respected. The people should have a say in what happens, and benefit when mining occurs.

This bauxite mine in the Northern Territory, Australia, is being restored and revegetated after mining.

This photo from 1998 shows how the forest was dying and the Ok Tedi river bed was 16.4 feet (5 m) higher due to a buildup of silt from the mine.

CASE STUDY
Mining at Ok Tedi

The Ok Tedi mine is situated at the headwaters of the Ok Tedi River, on Mount Fubilon, Papua New Guinea (PNG). In the 1980s and 1990s, the Ok Tedi mine hit the headlines because of the environmental damage from mining and its effects on the Min people. Today, the company running Ok Tedi is working with the people to build a sustainable future with the wealth from mining the area.

About the people

For more than 15,000 years, people have lived off the land, hunting, gathering, and farming in the mountains of New Guinea. There was virtually no contact with the outside world until recent times. Today, people live mainly in village communities.

The mine

When the American mining company Kennecott began mining copper at Ok Tedi in 1984, the environmental problems created, including pollution of the Ok Tedi River by silt and chemicals, made the headlines in papers around the world.

In 2002, the mine was handed back to PNG and a group of mining companies (OTML). Today, most of the 2,000 employees are PNG nationals, many from the local area. The mine now provides jobs, services, education, and health to the area and the environment is considered more.

Fast fact

In 2004, export sales from Ok Tedi made about 25 percent of PNG's exports.

Lumber and trees

Lumber is a valuable natural resource with many uses. Lumber is widely used for buildings, furniture, paper, crates, coffins, plywood sheets, chopsticks, household utensils, and many other items.

Many tree **species** are taken for lumber supplies by logging or chopping down the trees. Lumber is a **renewable** resource when it is growing faster than it is used.

The supply of lumber

Lumber comes from trees and trees grow. So in theory lumber is a sustainable, renewable resource. However, trees take time to grow. When more lumber is harvested than is grown, the supply is not sustainable.

Nowhere near enough trees are being planted to replace the current harvests to keep up with demand. Worldwide, huge areas of forest are being logged and **clear-felled** for lumber and paper.

Fast fact
Worldwide, only about 5 percent of forests are in protected areas, such as national parks, where no produce is removed.

These harvested trees will be made into paper.

Modern logging of Indonesian forests is not sustainable, and forests are disappearing quickly.

CASE STUDY
Logging in Indonesia

Today, huge areas of Indonesian rain forest are being destroyed by logging. Improved harvesting technology and increased demand for cheap lumber has increased the scale of logging and clear-felling in Indonesian forests. Much of the product is sold in the United States, Europe, China, and Japan.

Early logging

Before the 1960s, loggers usually took only single large, valuable trees. Individual trees were felled and their trunks dragged through the forest. This left the leaves and branches to decompose naturally. Overall, environmental disturbance was fairly low or similar in scale to natural events, such as tree death.

Fast fact
Between 1990 and 2005, Indonesia lost over 69 million acres (28 million ha) of forest, more than 30 percent of the country's forest cover, largely due to logging.

Modern logging

Valuable tree species, such as ramin, are fast disappearing from Indonesian forests due to overuse and modern logging techniques. Clear-felling, where all trees are removed from an area, prevents regrowth after harvest. The large areas that are opened up do not provide the right conditions for forest species to regrow. Today, almost all plant cover is taken, even very young trees.

Toward a sustainable future: Continuous lumber supply

The use of plantation lumber is the best way to provide a continuous lumber supply. Plantation lumber is trees planted and grown on farms. Given the decline of forests across the globe, this would not only provide lumber but also reduce **deforestation**. Recycling of already harvested lumber and paper products can also help with supply.

Fast fact

After damage by logging, the Indonesian islands were swept by extraordinary wildfires in the summer of 1998, damaging large areas and causing severe pollution.

Controlling forest harvests

Most of the rain forest lumber on the international market is exported to rich countries. There it is sold for hundreds of times the price that is paid to the **indigenous people** whose forests are destroyed. Cutting off this market for rain forest lumber would put an end to this destruction. Controls are needed to prevent sale of items made from illegal or unsustainable lumber supplies.

Sustainable harvests

Lumber grown in plantations must replace wild harvesting from natural forests. Growing lumber as a plantation crop to be harvested is the only way to sustain lumber supplies into the future. Increased planting of trees to harvest is urgent now, as trees take time to grow.

Plantation lumber can replace the collection of lumber from natural forests.

Paper and cardboard can be collected for recycling.

CASE STUDY
Recycling paper

Paper (and other lumber products) can be reused and recycled to help satisfy the demand for lumber. Packaging and newspapers are collected and recycled in many places throughout the world.

Importance of paper

Paper plays an important part in our everyday lives. Cheap and widely available paper helps increase literacy and the education of people throughout the world.

Reducing demand with recycling

More and more paper is today being collected for recycling. The reusing and recycling of made paper items contributes significantly to the supply of paper products. An important way to reduce demand for lumber is to reuse and recycle all items and products made from lumber.

ISSUE 3

Fast fact
In 1996, the World Resources Institute ranked commercial logging as the biggest cause of tropical rain forest decline.

19

Loss of good soil

Today, soil is being lost at a rapid rate across the globe. Productive soil is vital to grow plants, which provide many resources including lumber and food.

Land is being made unproductive by:
- erosion of the soil by wind and water
- salinity, where the soil contains so much salt it can no longer grow crops
- **desertification** due to loss of plant cover
- loss of nutrients

Fast fact

Every year, farmers abandon 27,000 square miles (70,000 sq km) of formerly productive land because the soil no longer supports crops.

What is soil?

Soil is not just dirt. Soil is a complex mixture of rock, air, water, fungi, bacteria, and **humus** that covers the surface of the land. Soil forms slowly and continuously by natural processes. Soil can therefore be described as a renewable resource.

Soil degradation and erosion

Misuse in the past has led to large-scale damage to soil, including loss of the fertile top layers. Misuses of soil include mining, bad farming techniques, overgrazing, deforestation, building, wars, pollution, and fires. Since 1945, around 10 percent of Earth's land, about 4.6 million square miles (12 million sq km) has been degraded.

Although the importance of soil has been known for a very long time, soil erosion continues today at an increasing rate.

Healthy soil is vital in the production of most food crops.

A dust storm approaches the town of Stratford, Texas, in the 1930s.

CASE STUDY
The American Dust Bowl

One of the most well described cases of soil erosion was in the Midwest region of the United States, in the 1930s. The "Dust Bowl" occurred when large areas were so severely eroded that the whole topsoil blew away.

The Dust Bowl

The Dust Bowl area included parts of Kansas, Oklahoma, Texas, New Mexico, and Colorado. In its natural state, the region was covered with hardy grasses that held the fine-grained soil in place, despite long droughts and occasional torrential rains. A large number of farmers settled in the region after the 1880s.

Farming

Planting wheat and raising cattle left the soil exposed. The winds that constantly swept over the gently rolling land combined with a period of severe drought and the soil began to blow away. Erosion was so bad that farms were abandoned.

Fast fact
On April 14, 1935, known as "Black Sunday," day turned into night as a dust storm carried away millions of tons of precious soil.

ISSUE 4

21

Toward a sustainable future: Managing the land

Soil is a precious renewable natural resource that needs to be conserved. Today, **land management** techniques involve caring for soil so it can continue to provide for us in the future.

Soil conservation

Soil conservation means taking steps to keep soil in place and keep it productive. In many countries, retaining healthy forest cover and finding better ways of grazing and planting are helping hold soil together. Reducing the loss of soil and speeding up soil formation can help renew this valuable resource.

Farming the soil

Sustainable soil use means farming in ways that put into the soil as many nutrients as are taken out. Fragile soil must be disturbed as little as possible. Farm machinery can break up the soil's structure, making it less fertile. Many natural methods to help maintain and increase soil and its fertility are being investigated and used in **organic farming**.

Fast fact
Demand for food worldwide by the year 2050 will be about three times current levels.

Food needs to be grown in ways that care for the soil so it can continue to provide crops in the future.

This organic farm, in California, grows a mixture of vegetables in a way that enriches the soil, rather than intensively farming one type of crop in a way that depletes the soil.

CASE STUDY
Organic farming

Organic farming methods keep keep the soil in place and also make it more fertile. Today, organic farming is more widely accepted as better for the soil and for production of vital resources.

As much as possible, organic farmers work with natural materials to increase productivity. Organic farming avoids or excludes the use of **artificial fertilizers**, pesticides, growth regulators, and feed additives. Disturbance of the soil is kept to a minimum.

Organic techniques

Organic farming techniques include:

- changing or rotating crops rather than growing the same crop all the time, to help prevent disease and enrich soil
- composting animal manure and plant material left after harvesting
- growing plants to increase fertility, such as peas which increase nitrogen in the soil
- using natural predators rather than chemicals to control pests and weeds

Resources going to waste

Huge amounts of trash and garbage can be seen just about anywhere in the world. The idea of throwing away what is no longer wanted as garbage is causing enormous environmental problems.

What is garbage?

Garbage is any disposed of, unwanted material. In the past, much less garbage was created than today. This is because there were fewer people, and resources were harder to come by. In the past, almost all waste was biodegradable—it would break down and, under the right conditions, add to soil fertility.

Landfill sites

Fast fact

Today's garbage contains many nonbiodegradable plastics. These plastics do not break down with time, remaining in the soil for many thousands of years.

Landfill is one of the main ways trash has been disposed of throughout history. Every day, huge amounts of daily waste are taken away to a landfill for disposal. New landfill sites are becoming difficult to find. Many toxic substances in today's waste are being released into the soil in landfills.

Huge areas of land are taken up by trash.

Garbage piles up during the Athens garbage collectors' strike.

CASE STUDY
Garbage piling up in Athens

The amount of garbage created often goes unnoticed. A series of strikes by garbage collectors in Athens led to more than 40,000 tons of garbage becoming very visible, sitting rotting in the streets. Athens, a Greek city with four million people, produces about 5,500 tons of garbage each day, which is usually collected and disposed of in landfills.

Rotting garbage

Athenians continued to dump more than 1,500 tons of garbage a day during the strike while garbage on the streets became putrid. One woman, Eleni, told the British broadcaster BBC, "We think that it's horrible, it's disgusting, there is an unbearable smell everywhere. We are terrified that diseases might spread everywhere. We have to shut doors, to close windows, so that no fly or mosquito gets in the flat. It's a horror."

Garbage disposal

Today, most garbage in Greece goes to landfills, although more recycling is planned. In 2003, there were 1,032 dumping sites still operating throughout Greece. Plans to recycle the estimated 750,000 tons of packaging materials (glass, plastic, metal, and paper) that Greeks throw away every year are well behind schedule.

> **Fast fact**
> Leaders in ancient Athens required all household garbage to be buried at least 1 mile (1.6 km) from town. Just like today, finding good dump sites was difficult.

25

Toward a sustainable future: Garbage as a resource

Using waste as a resource is important to a more sustainable future. Techniques have now been developed to reuse or recycle all "garbage" into useful products. Reusing and recycling turns garbage into a resource rather than seeing it as a problem.

Sorting waste

Until recently, most recycling of waste required sorting out paper, metal, glass, and plastic. After years of separating for recycling, many cities are now developing ways of recycling using just one bin, called "single-stream" recycling. This method of collection makes recycling more popular and less expensive. Single-stream programs show a doubling of recycling rates.

Zero waste

The environmental group Greenpeace is supporting "zero waste" as the target for a sustainable future. For instance, Kamikatsu province in Japan is planning for zero waste by 2020. Currently, this area disposes of garbage in landfills and by high-temperature burning. The eventual aim must be to develop zero waste approaches worldwide.

Fast fact

In 2005, recycling in suburbs of Philadelphia increased when people were given vouchers to local shops when they separated their recycling from other waste.

This recycling collection center has bins for plastic, paper, metal, and glass.

CASE STUDY

Garbage as a resource in Indonesia

A project in Sukunan village, Indonesia, is a good example of decreasing trash and garbage problems by thinking of garbage as a resource. This local program is the first of its type anywhere in Indonesia.

Sukunan village garbage

Sukunan village, on the outskirts of Yogyakarta, has an increasing population. With no place for garbage or garbage collection, litter was an extreme problem. Every household disposed of its own trash and many people did not realize plastic would not break down. The farmers complained because plastic clogged up their paddy fields, reducing rice yields.

Recycling the resource

Iswanto, a Sukunan resident, started the project after seeing the way Australians working in the area approached the garbage problem. He experimented with separating paper and plastic, and making compost out of household waste. Soon his neighbors followed his example. The process spread throughout the area, which now has colorful collection bins as a feature and gets income from recycling projects.

What can you do?
Save natural resources

You may think that just one person cannot do much, but everyone can help. If every person is careful, the little differences can add up.

Reduce your garbage

Households produce garbage every day. Think carefully when purchasing items. You may be able to reuse and recycle to help decrease the garbage problem and save resources.

Reduce

Simple actions can reduce consumption of resources and production of waste. Think about what you are doing as you do it, with the goal of reducing consumption in mind.

Reuse

Reusing is use of the same item more than once, preferably many times, rather than disposal after one use. When shopping, avoid products that are designed to be thrown away. Reuse plastic bags that come home with you.

Recycle

Glass, paper, metal, and plastic can be recycled in manufactured goods. **Organic waste** can be composted. Recycling can also occur when we shop, by choosing products with recycled packaging or made from recycled material.

Fast fact
You can make your own handmade recycled paper from waste paper.

Composting your kitchen scraps is a great way to turn garbage into a useful resource.

Analyze your garbage

How much trash do you throw away? Analyzing your own garbage is part of the process of valuing resources.

What to do

Begin by sorting your garbage each day into these five groups:

- organic waste
- paper
- plastic
- glass
- metal

Weigh each group at the end of each day and answer these questions:

- How much do you have of each group?
- What is the biggest contributor to waste that cannot be recycled?
- How much of this garbage could be eliminated by changing your shopping habits?

Toward a sustainable future

Well, I hope you now see that if you accept my challenge your world will be a better place. There are many ways to work toward a sustainable future. Imagine it . . . a world with:

- a stable climate
- clean air and water
- nonpolluting, renewable fuel supplies
- plenty of food
- resources for everyone
- healthy natural environments

This is what you can achieve if you work together with my natural systems.

We must work together to live sustainably. That will mean a better environment and a better life for all living things on Earth, now and in the future.

Web sites

For further information on natural resources, visit these Web sites:

- Planet Ark www.planetark.com
- Recycling www.newstarget.com/006186.html
- Ok Tedi mine www.oktedi.com/aboutus/
- International Buy Nothing Day www.adbusters.org

Glossary

artificial fertilizers
chemical fertilizers made by people, rather than natural fertilizers such as animal manure

clear-felled
the removal of all trees from an area

climate change
changes to the usual weather patterns in an area

consumption
amount used or consumed

deforestation
removal or clearing of forest cover

degraded
run down or reduced to a lower quality

desertification
turning an area into desert, with low plant cover and a high risk of erosion

developed countries
countries with industrial development, a strong economy, and a high standard of living

erosion
process of rock and soil being carried away by wind and water

fossil fuels
fuels such as oil, coal, and gas, which formed underground from the remains of animals and plants that lived millions of years ago

global warming
an increase in the average temperature on Earth

humus
broken down material from living things

indigenous people
the first inhabitants of a particular area

landfill
areas of land where waste is dumped

land management
organizing and controlling ways in which land is used

nonrenewable
a resource that is limited in supply and which cannot be replaced once it runs out

ore
natural form of metals in the ground

organic farming
method of farming that tries to make the soil more fertile without using artificial fertilizers, pesticides, or other chemicals

organic waste
waste from living things, such as vegetable peelings

raw materials
unprocessed materials from which other things are made

recycling
reprocessing a material so that it can be used again

renewable
a resource that can be constantly supplied and which does not run out

species
living things of the same grouping

sustainable
a way of living that does not use up natural resources

United Nations Environment Program
a program, which is part of the United Nations, set up to encourage nations to care for the environment

World Resources Institute
a United States nongovernment organization set up to find solutions to serious global environmental problems

Index